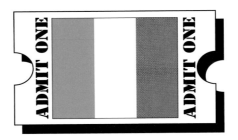

Johnstown Castle, Former Home To Wealthy Families

IRELAND

BY PATRICK RYAN

THE CHILD'S WORLD®, INC.

9510122

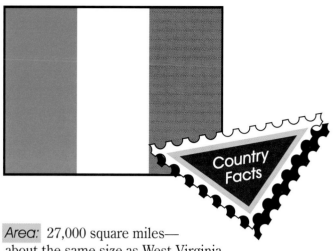

Area: 27,000 square miles—
about the same size as West Virginia.

Population: About 4 million people.

Capital City: Dublin.

Other Important Cities: Cork, Limerick.

Money: The Irish pound.

National Languages: English and Gaelic.

National Holiday: New Years Day on January 1.

National Song: "Amhran ha BhFiann," or "The Soldier's Song."

National Flag: Three stripes of green, white and orange.

Head of Government: The president of Ireland.

Text copyright © 2000 by The Child's World®, Inc.
All rights reserved. No part of this book may be reproduced
or utilized in any form or by any means without written
permission from the publisher.
Printed in the United States of America.

Library of Congress Cataloging-in-Publication Data
Ryan, Pat (Patrick M.)
Ireland / by Patrick Ryan
Series: "Faces and Places".
p. cm.
Includes index.
Summary: Describes the geography, history,
people and customs of Ireland.
ISBN 1-56766-599-3 (library : reinforced : alk. paper)

1. Ireland — Juvenile literature.
[1. Ireland] I. Title.

DA906.R93 1999
941.5 — dc21   98-45689
                                               CIP
                                               AC

GRAPHIC DESIGN
Robert A. Honey, Seattle

PHOTO RESEARCH
James R. Rothaus / James R. Rothaus & Associates

ELECTRONIC PRE-PRESS PRODUCTION
Robert E. Bonaker / Graphic Design & Consulting Co.

PHOTOGRAPHY
Cover photo: Irish Schoolgirl With Doll
by Paul A. Souders/Corbis

Table of Contents

Imagine you are on a jet airplane. From high above Earth, you would notice that some of the land areas are very large. These pieces of land are called **continents.** Other land areas are much smaller. Some pieces of land are surrounded by water on all sides. These are called **islands**.

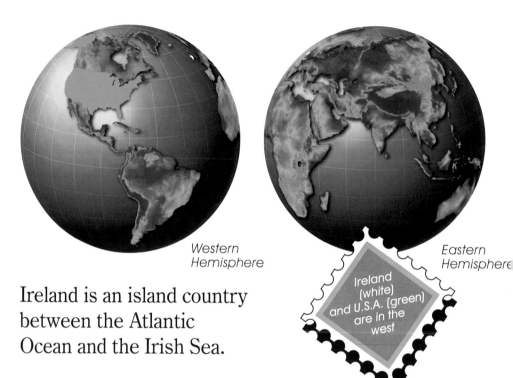

Western Hemisphere

Eastern Hemisphere

Ireland (white) and U.S.A. (green) are in the west

Ireland is an island country between the Atlantic Ocean and the Irish Sea.

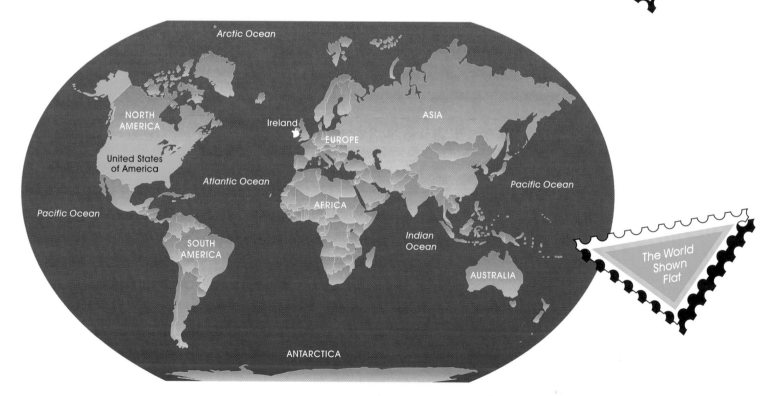

Arctic Ocean

NORTH AMERICA

ASIA

Ireland

EUROPE

United States of America

Atlantic Ocean

Pacific Ocean

Pacific Ocean

AFRICA

SOUTH AMERICA

Indian Ocean

AUSTRALIA

ANTARCTICA

The World Shown Flat

6

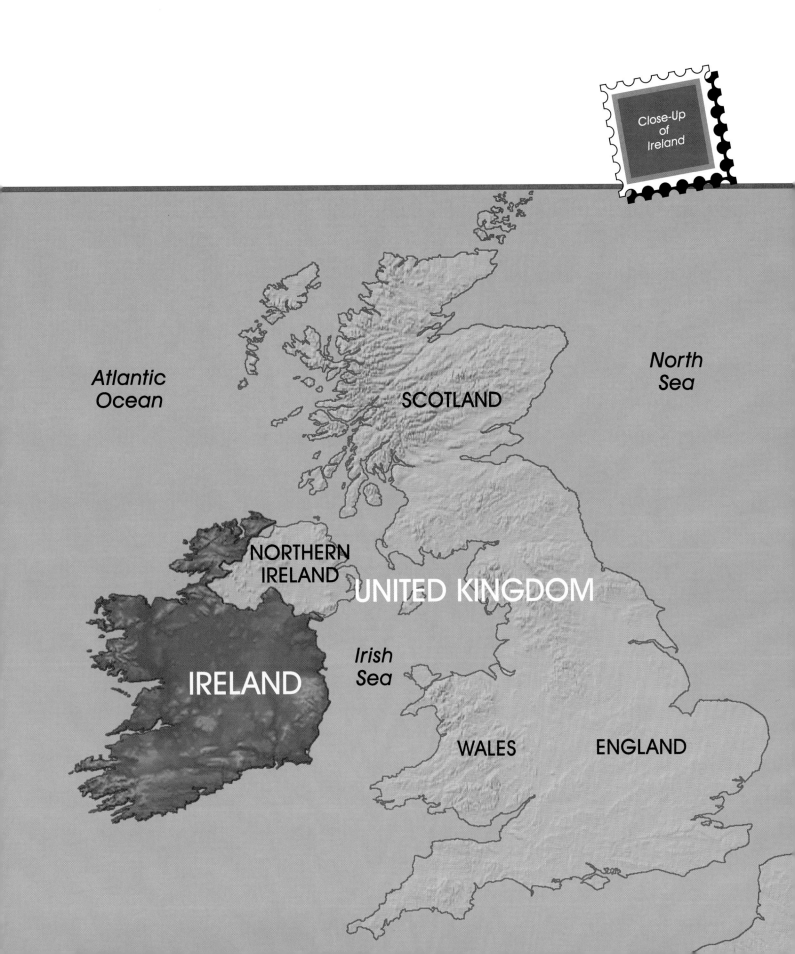

Close-Up
of
Ireland

*Atlantic
Ocean*

*North
Sea*

SCOTLAND

NORTHERN
IRELAND

UNITED KINGDOM

*Irish
Sea*

IRELAND

WALES

ENGLAND

The Cong
River And
Lough
Corrib

Cong River
Lough Corrib

Cliffs of Moher

Newcastle ●

Johnstown Castle ■

Wicklow Mountains

Kit Kittle/Corbis

Massive Cliffs
Of Moher

Michael St. Maur Sheil/Corbis

Ireland is often called the "Emerald Isle." It got its nickname from its green hills and valleys. At different times of the year, it rains almost every day in Ireland. Some people believe the tiny island has 40 shades of green.

Richard Cummins/Corbis

Autumn
Leaves And
Forest Near
Wicklow
Mountains

Ireland is a beautiful country. It has rolling hills, quiet meadows and tall, rocky cliffs. There are thick forests and breezy beaches, too.

Hills
And Valleys
Near
Newcastle

Richard Cummins/Corbis

9

Ireland's mild weather and constant rainfall make it the perfect place for many types of plants and trees to grow. In many areas, green grasses and wildflowers live. Forests of trees such as oak and pine grow well, too.

Most of the animals in Ireland are small creatures such as foxes, badgers, and rabbits. Hedgehogs, which look like tiny porcupines, can sometimes be seen walking along the roads. Ireland's most treasured creatures live in the cold country streams. Brown trout and rainbow trout are common in these areas. So are herring, cod, mackerel, and salmon. In fact, people from all over the world come to Ireland to fish in these beautiful spots.

Coastal Wildflowers Of Dunmore East

Ricahrd Cummins/Corbis

Michael St. Maur Sheil/Corbis

Pony From Connemara National Park

Sheep On A Grassy Slope Near Portnablagh

Tom Bean/Corbis

Portnablagh

Connemara
National Park

Ardagh

Dunmore East

George McCarthy/Corbis

Hedgehog
Near The Town
Of Ardagh

Muckross House (1448) Was Set Afire By Englishmen In 1652

Clonmacnoise

Muckross House ■ ■ Cahir Castle

Rosscarbery

Richard Cummins/Corbis

Cahir Castle Was Built 600 Years Ago

Richard Cummins/Corbis

People have been living in Ireland for thousands of years. Some people came to Ireland by walking. That's because long ago, the oceans were lower than they are now. Many continents were connected together by land areas called **land bridges**. Over the years, the waters rose and covered up the bridges. That is how Ireland became an island!

Over time, other groups came to Ireland by boat. One group, called the **Celts** (KELTS), were fierce warriors. They lived in small kingdoms all across Ireland. Many of the Celtic kingdoms fought against each other over different land areas.

More than 800 years ago, explorers from the country of Great Britain visited Ireland. They told their king about the beautiful green island. The king wanted Ireland to be part of his kingdom. Some of the Irish people thought that Great Britain would be a good ruler. Other people thought that Ireland should be its own country. For many years, the English and Irish people fought over who should rule the country.

Stone Pillars From Rosscarbery Are About 3,200 Years Old

Richard Cummins/Corbis

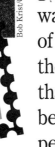
Celtic Crosses At Ancient Center Of Clonmacnoise

Bob Krist/Corbis

Eamon De Valera Was The Republic Of Ireland's First President

Hulton-Deutsh Collection/Corbis

From 1840 to 1845, Ireland's main crop, the potato, did not grow well—or even at all! Without food, many of the Irish people starved. Others left Ireland for America to escape the pain and suffering. This hard time was called the **Potato Famine**.

For years, many Irish people struggled. They had very little money and food. Many people thought that Great Britain was not helping the Irish people enough. To help Ireland become stronger, the Irish felt they needed to be rulers of their own country. After years of fighting and talking, Ireland separated from Great Britain in 1921. But Great Britain did not want to give up the whole island. Instead, Great Britain held onto the very northern part of Ireland. Great Britain still rules northern Ireland today.

Englishman, Sir Charles Trevelyan Ran The Relief Works During 1840 Famine

Trouble In Dublin During Irish War Of Independence (1921)

Sean Sexton Collection/Corbis

Sean Sexton Collection/Corbis

NORTHERN IRELAND

Dublin ☆

Dublin's Parliament Building

Michael Nicholson/Corbis

A Family
Shares
A Joke
In Dingle

Milltown Malbay

Dingle

Wicklow

Blarney

Macduff Everton/Corbis

GUINNESS
IS GOOD
FOR YOU

DAN FOLEY

Local Men Entertain Friends In Milltown Malbay

Stephanie Maze/Corbis

Only about four million people live in Ireland. Most are relatives of the Celts. Others are relatives of the settlers from Great Britain. Some people are relatives of both.

The Irish people are known all over the world for their kindness. They are happy and gentle, and love to talk with family and friends. In fact, one of the most popular things to do in Ireland is to talk! The Irish people love to tell stories, and tell jokes. They often will sit for hours and talk about everything from the government to fishing.

Tim Thompson/Corbis

Bend Backwards, Kiss The Blarney Stone, Get The Gift Of Gab

Friends Having Fun In Wicklow

Tim Thompson/Corbis

City Life And Country Life

Most of the Irish people live in cities or towns. In big cities there are hotels, shops, restaurants, and factories. There is at least one train station, too. Most city people live in small apartment buildings called **flats**. Others live in small houses with little yards.

Colorful Irish Row Houses In Eyeries

Richard Cummins/Corbis

Michael S. Yamashita/Corbis

Farmhouses And Rock Walls On Inisheer Island

In the country, Irish people live in small houses called **cottages**. They farm the green land or raise animals such as cows, sheep, or horses.

Old Irish Cottage In Leenane

Richard Cummins/Corbis

Leenane •
ARAN ISLANDS
Inisheer Island

Mount Juliet House
Eyeries •

Tony Roberts/Corbis

Mount
Juliet
House
And Horse
Farm

Kylemore
Abbey Is
Home To
A Girls'
School

Kylemore Abbey ■
Lahinch •
Dublin ☆ Trinity College
Blarney •

Ric Ergenbright/Corbis

Schools And Language

In Ireland, boys and girls go to school until they are 16 years old. They learn things such as math, writing, and reading. They also learn *Gaelic* (GAY–lik). Gaelic is the oldest language in Ireland.

Irish children wear uniforms to school. In the country, some schools only have one room and one teacher. In these areas, students from different grades all learn in the same classroom.

Trinity College In Dublin Has Very Old Books

Michael St. Maur Sheil/Corbis

Students Outside School In Blarney

Kelly-Mooney Photography/Corbis

ag léim

Stephanie Maze/Corbis

Children Learning Gaelic In Lahinch

Work

One important job in Ireland is **tourism**. In this job, the Irish people show visitors from other countries about Ireland. Each year, millions of people come to Ireland to learn about the people of long ago and see their castles. They also come to meet the Irish people, listen to their stories, and see their beautiful, green land.

Farming is also a very important job in Ireland. Many of the green meadows are used to raise animals such as sheep. In fact, there are more sheep in Ireland than people! The wool from the sheep is spun into yarn that is used for sweaters and other types of warm clothing.

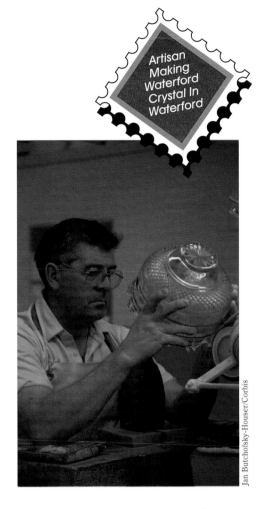

Artisan Making Waterford Crystal In Waterford

Jan Butchofsky-Houser/Corbis

Hostess Serves Tea At Newport House In Newport

Macduff Everton/Corbis

Dingle Peninsula Tourists In Wagon, Meet Sheep On Road

Macduff Everton/Corbis

Michael St. Maur Sheil/Corbis

Killybegs

Newport

Dingle
Peninsula

Waterford

Unloading
Fish At
Killybegs
Harbor

Dining At
Ashford
Castle

Ashford Castle
Portumna
Ballymaloe House
Schull

Macduff Everton/Corbis

Bread And Cheese From Gubbeen House In Schull

Michael St. Maur Sheil/Corbis

Meal time is a special time for the Irish. Everyone comes together to talk, laugh and eat. Most meals contain at least one dish that is made with potatoes. *Irish stew*, a dish made with lamb, onions, and potatoes, is a traditional favorite.

Another popular food in Ireland is bread. The Irish have dozens of different breads that they like to make. They like to drink tea, too. Foods such as hamburgers, fries, and pizza are also popular in the bigger cities.

Tea Time At The Ballymaloe House Hotel

Catherine Karnow/Corbis

Boys Eating Popsicles Outside A Store In Portumna

Bob Krist/Corbis

The Irish love to sing, dance, and read. They like to play outdoors and go on long walks. They also have many favorite sports. The green meadows of Ireland are the perfect place for a game called **hurling**. Hurling is played with sticks and a ball. The players try to hit the ball into a goal. Hurling is a little like the game of *lacrosse*.

Irish football or Gaelic football is another popular game. It's like soccer, except the players can catch the ball with their hands and run. At the end of the field, players try to kick the ball through tall poles.

Irish Folk Dancers At A Fair In Skibbereen

Tim Thompson/Corbis

Rugby Cup Finals In Galway

Fishing The Shannon River Is A Great Pastime

Bob Krist/Corbis

Michael St. Maur Sheil/Corbis

Galway

Shannon River

Ennis

Skibbereen

Stephanie Maze/Corbis

Friends Practicing Hurling In Ennis

Choir On Croagh Patrick Where St. Patrick Banished The Reptiles

Croagh Patrick

Dublin ☆

Adare

Dungarvan

Michael St. Maur Sheil/Corbis

Holidays

ADMIT ONE · ADMIT ONE

Many of the holidays in Ireland are religious. Christmas and Easter are two religious holidays that most Irish people celebrate. St. Patrick's Day is also an important religious holiday in Ireland. The Irish also have government holidays. "Bank holidays" are holidays when people do not have to go to work. Instead, many travel to different areas or stay home and relax.

The gentle, green hills of Ireland make it one of the most beautiful places in the world. Ireland is also a country with a rich history. It has many interesting sites to visit. The kind people make Ireland one of the nicest places, too. If you get the chance to visit Ireland, make sure you're ready to listen—the Irish are ready to tell you some wonderful stories!

Woman Sells Flowers For The Holidays In Dublin

Catherine Karnow/Corbis

This Castle In Dungarvan Is Visited By People On Holidays

Paul Almasy/Corbis

29

Adare
Country
Cottage
With
Thatched
Roof

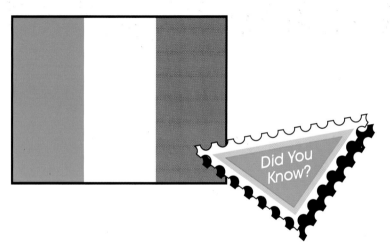

Did You Know?

Many people visit Blarney Castle in southern Ireland. At the castle, many people lean backwards to kiss a smooth stone in the castle's wall. Legend has it that people who kiss this rock, called the Blarney Stone, are able to talk about anything to anyone.

Some country homes in Ireland are heated with **peat**. Peat is made from rotting marsh plants. Country people scoop the peat out of marshes and then burn the peat in their fireplaces or stoves.

Ireland is home to some of the tallest cliffs in Europe. The Cliffs of Moher on Ireland's west coast are 700 feet high.

On happy occasions, Irish people like to dance jigs and reels. They kick their feet high as happy music plays. These dances look a little like American square dancing.

How Do You Say?

	GAELIC	HOW TO SAY IT
Hello	dia duit	(DEE–uh git)
Goodbye	slán agat	(SLAWN uh–guht)
Please	más é do thoil é	(maw–shay–duh–HILL–ay)
Thank You	go raibh maith agat	(guh–ruh–MAH–huh–guht)
One	a haon	(uh HAY–nn)
Two	a dó	(uh DOH)
Three	a trí	(uh TREE)
Ireland	Éire	(AY–er)

Glossary

continents (KON–tih–nents)
Most of the land areas on Earth are divided up into huge sections called continents. Some continents contain many countries.

cottages (KAH–tuh–jez)
Country homes in Ireland are often called cottages.

Celts (KELTS)
The Celts were one of the first groups of people to live in Ireland. The Celts were known as fierce warriors.

hurling (HUR–ling)
Hurling is a sport that many Irish like to play. Hurling is a little like the game of lacrosse.

island (EYE–land)
An island is an area of land that has water on all sides. Ireland is an island.

flats (FLATS)
Flats are small apartment buildings in Ireland. Many city people in Ireland live in flats.

land bridges (LAND BRIH–jez)
Land bridges are areas of land that connect two continents together. Long ago, people crossed land bridges from Europe to Ireland.

peat (PEET)
Peat is the decayed parts of marsh plants. Some country people use peat to heat their homes.

Potato Famine (poh–TAY–to FA–min)
The Potato Famine was a time when much of Ireland's potato crop did not grow well. Many people became very poor and starved during the Potato Famine.

tourism (TOOR–ih–zem)
The business of showing travelers around a country is called tourism. Tourism is a very important business in Ireland.

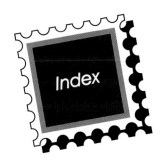

Index